Also by Peter Magubane

MAGUBANE'S SOUTH AFRICA

BLACK
CHILD

BLACK
CHILD

Peter Magubane

ALFRED A. KNOPF   NEW YORK 1982

THIS IS A BORZOI BOOK
PUBLISHED BY ALFRED A. KNOPF, INC.

Copyright © 1982 by Peter Magubane
All rights reserved under International and Pan-American
Copyright Conventions. Published in the United States
by Alfred A. Knopf, Inc., New York, and simultaneously
in Canada by Random House of Canada Limited, Toronto.
Distributed by Random House, Inc., New York.

Library of Congress Cataloging in Publication Data

Magubane, Peter.   Black child.

1. Blacks—South Africa—Social conditions—Pictorial
works.   2. Children, Black—South Africa—Social
conditions—Pictorial works.   3. South Africa—Social
conditions—1961-   —Pictorial works.   I. Title.
DT763.6.M33   968'.00496   81-48102
ISBN 0-394-51445-9   AACR2
ISBN 0-394-70959-4 (pbk.)

Manufactured in the United States of America
First Edition

12587709

I dedicate this book to Sir Thomas Hopkinson—former editor of *Picture Post* in London, and of *Drum Magazine* in South Africa from 1957 until his resignation in 1961—and to my dearest friend, Nathanial Nakasa, who died in New York in 1965.

I am grateful to Rose Catchings and Ron Stoner of the Methodist Board of Global Ministries for their help with this project. I am also grateful to two special people who helped with the editing and typing of the manuscript, Vivian Grice and Bertha Jones.

BLACK
CHILD

I am writing as a black photojournalist very concerned about the plight of the black child in South Africa. I had hoped that things would have changed for the better by the time this book was published, but instead they have gone from bad to worse. It grieves me that I will not be singing praises of my country, South Africa, but must write instead about the sadness of my experiences involving black children during the twenty-six years of my journalistic career. I will nevertheless try to give an unbiased picture.

To review the situation in my country is a nightmarish job, for no other nation is as troubled and tense as South Africa today. A country that has been fighting oppression for the past three hundred years can only have very complicated and unique problems.

For the history of the blacks in South Africa the period from June 16, 1976, until now may have been the most important span of time since the arrival of the white man. On the one hand, the South African government sees it as the culmination of the Verwoerdian dream of separate development, as "independence" has been given to black tribal territories such as the Transkei. On the other hand, this period marks the beginning of an internal struggle led mostly by children from age twelve on. In the later stages, even younger children, in primary school, became involved. South Africa was bathed in blood, torn by riots, with deaths estimated at as high as 1,000, or—officially—at 575.

The upheavals began with a children's revolt. On June 16, 1976, about 20,000 students staged a demonstration against the abhorred Bantu educational policy. It is abhorred because of its deliberate inferiority and because it is tailored by whites for our children, although black educators exist who could be responsible for black education. And why should there be different educational systems for people in one country?

The explosive issue was that of the Afrikaans language. Blacks in secondary schools used to be taught in English, but in 1974 the South African government ruled that at least half of all subjects had to be taught in Afrikaans, the language of the most hated and reactionary section of the whites. Because there was so much resistance to the ruling from teachers, school boards, administrators, and students, it was not widely enforced at first. When it was enforced, two years later, there was trouble. On June 10, 1976, students in the black Johannesburg section called Soweto refused to write a social study paper in Afrikaans, and the following day, at the Morris Isaacson School, they boycotted classes.

On June 16, at the instigation of the Soweto Students' Representative Council, students from different schools in the whole Soweto complex marched to a central point to discuss their grievances and decide what action should be taken. They carried placards made out of cardboard boxes bearing such slogans as: "Down with Afrikaans," "Afrikaans is a tribal language," "Afrikaans is the oppressors' language," "Afrikaans stinks and it is the most dangerous drug for our future." The march was peaceful. But at 10:30 a.m., thirteen-year-old Hector Peterson was fatally wounded by the police, who opened fire and threw tear-gas cannisters at the children outside the Orlando West Junior High School. This caused the smoldering anger of years to erupt with unimaginable venom. The students ran amok. I am convinced that the situation could have been contained had it not been for the interference of the police, which aggravated a potentially explosive situation. This was the beginning of unrest throughout the whole of South Africa.

A white official was clubbed to death that morning, apparently in revenge. Police retaliated with more reinforcements, and for the first time Soweto had camouflaged police arriving in vans. The children regrouped and sang the national anthem "Nkosi Sikeleli Africa"—"God Bless Africa." Meanwhile, nearly all the offices of the Bantu administration in Soweto were attacked and burned down, along with post offices, beer halls and liquor stores (the last are government property and its major source of income in the black areas). Slogans appeared on walls and the students shouted them: "Less liquor, better education, more schools and less beer halls." Police reinforcements poured into Soweto. By midday the whole township was out of control. Soweto was ablaze. The Minister of Justice, Police and Prisons, Jimmy Kruger, encouraged the white vigilantes to kill if necessary to protect their property, saying of the children: "That's what they want, if their parents can't control them." Hundreds of children were detained, some of them as young as fifteen. More than 500 were charged, found guilty, and given sentences ranging from five years upwards. Many are today serving terms in the high-security prison on Robben Island, and hundreds have fled the country.

On June 18 the anger of the children erupted in the Alexandra Township, another black area near Johannesburg. They had received news of the Soweto unrest the day before. The West Rand Administration Board offices were badly damaged, and dozens of vehicles were set alight, including two Public Utility Transport Corporation buses. A huge roadblock was set up in the center of the township. Written in large letters across it were the words: WHY KILL CHILDREN FOR AFRIKAANS?

The police quickly set up headquarters in the damaged Administration Board office block. Meanwhile hundreds of riot squad police moved about the township armed with automatic weapons. The streets echoed to the sound of automatic fire and the screams of young children.

I saw young children and adults being fatally wounded. That day Alexandra looked like a battlefield.

Typically, the white minority government promptly put the blame on "known agitators." From a black point of view, it is hard to understand what exactly is meant by the term "agitator." When black leaders talk about the resentment of the black community and ask the people to stand up for their rights, in most cases the government automatically labels these leaders "agitators with no known following." It is just an excuse to detain them. South Africa was at that time expecting a visit from Henry Kissinger. Mr. John Vorster, the former Prime Minister, suggested that the "agitators" were hoping to gain international publicity by provoking a riot when Kissinger was on his way. He didn't seem to realize that the whole apartheid structure was on trial.

The Minister of Police's reaction to the chaos was to appoint Mr. Justice P. M. Cillié, the Judge President of the Supreme Court of the Transvaal, to conduct a one-man commission of inquiry into the causes of the riots. Black leaders were quick to point out that this commission would not serve any purpose if blacks were not represented on it. Yet their request was refused, and the government went further—it arrested the leading members of the Black People's Convention and the South African Students' Organization, as well as black journalists and photographers, and hundreds of children.

Whose fault was it? In 1980, Mr. Justice Cillié issued his report, a 760-page document, which, although it failed to point out how the police aggravated the riots, still delivered a damning judgment on the system. Mr. Cillié blamed the riots on apartheid and certain government policies that created dissatis-faction and hatred. The policies included Bantu Education, the Homeland system, influx control, and the Group Area Act, which gives the government legal power to set up separate residential areas, businesses and education for different ethnic groups. Other policies causing discontent included salary discrimination, labor restrictions and detention without trial. The report emphasized that discrimination had caused "great hate." In short, the cause of the riots was the apartheid system itself in all its manifestations.

The education system for black children was formulated in 1953 by Dr. Hendrik Verwoerd, then Minister of Native Affairs and later Prime Minister. In 1953, he told Parliament that "if the native [meaning the black in South Africa] today, in any kind of school in existence, is being taught to expect that he will live his adult life under a policy of equal rights, he is making a mistake."

Dr. Verwoerd introduced the Bantu Education Bill, which placed black education under one state department. Until then, black education, like that of other races, was under the control of the individual provinces. In his speech in Parliament, Dr. Verwoerd questioned the usefulness of teaching blacks about the kings of England and Canada's wheat exports, and added: "What is the use of teaching the Bantu child mathematics when it cannot use it in practice? That is quite absurd." Dr. Verwoerd went on:

> . . . if my department controls native education it will know for which types of higher profession the native can be trained, and where he will be able to use his knowledge to make a living. It will guide him, instead of allowing him to choose his own path in a direction where he cannot find a sphere of activity, thus becoming a frustrated and dissatisfied being. But apart from these persons who can serve their own people, there is the much greater number of natives who have to find a future in other forms of work. The latter should have a training in accordance with their opportunities in life, and no department will know better where and how great the opportunities are for the Bantu child.

It is this approach to education that still governs the schooling of blacks in South Africa. How long must these children suffer? How long is it going to take the government to realize that Bantu education overall is neither fair nor good for the black child and must be done away with? After all, this was what sparked off the June 1976 riots.

Although the bill became law, the debate on it in 1953 was heated. A Labor Party M.P., Mr. Leo Lovell, pointed out angrily that the real meaning of the bill was that black people were to be educated to become a commodity whose labor could be bought and sold "like a bag of corn."

One of the selling points of Dr. Verwoerd's program was economy: education was to be extended to all blacks without any increase of expenditure. This would be achieved by sticking to fundamentals—a knowledge of reading, writing and arithmetic, a sound knowledge of English, and a basic knowledge of Afrikaans. This was all the education he considered necessary for a black child. He was right that it would be economical; in 1980, the amount spent by the government for each black child's education was one-tenth the amount spent for a white child.

Another issue Dr. Verwoerd introduced during the same debate was that of control. He said that if the state paid for the Bantu's education, it should also control it. He forgot to consider that black parents also pay for Bantu education. Though their contributions may not cover the entire cost, many of them spend a large proportion of their earnings on the school fees which the government has always exacted from the parents of black—but not white—children in public schools.

Control was still an ideal twenty-three years later. On the day violence erupted in Soweto, Dr. Andries Treurnicht, Deputy Minister of Bantu Development and Education, told an Afrikaans newspaper that the policy that Afrikaans should be taught side by side with English in black schools had been applied with great tolerance. "In white areas where the government provides the buildings, gives the subsidies and pays the teachers, it is surely our right to decide on the language dispensation," he said. (By "white areas" he meant all those parts of South Africa that are not designated "Homelands." Soweto, though all its inhabitants are black, is part of a white area.) Dr. Treurnicht said he had been aware that dissatisfaction was brewing in Soweto; nobody knew better than the Afrikaner the dangers of forcing people to use a language. But it had been felt that a knowledge of both English and Afrikaans would be to the pupils' advantage.

Since the riots, black schools have been permitted not to use Afrikaans as a medium of instruction, though it is still a compulsory subject of study. But the government has moved to make further protests more difficult. A new Education and Training Act, passed in 1980 and to be implemented gradually beginning in 1981, will make education for blacks compulsory, though still not free. The act is designed to shift the role of containing the restlessness of black youth from police to parents. Parents and guardians who fail to ensure their children's attendance at school will be liable to a fine or imprisonment. Parents, already burdened with school fees, will hardly be able to afford to flout the law.

So far, boycotting classes has been the best means of protest available to students. Now that the consequences of their actions will be borne by their families as well as themselves, their political activity will inevitably be restricted.

The Education and Training Act was passed in spite of the opposition of educators like Professor Michael Ashly, Dean of the Educational Faculty at the University of Cape Town, who disagrees strongly with making education compulsory at this point when the grievances that underlay the boycott are still unresolved. He believes that compulsory education should not be introduced until at least 90 percent of the children who would be affected by it are already enrolled in school. Instead of making education compulsory in the present unsettled climate and thereby risking political confrontation, the department ought to concentrate on building up the system. This would include new schools and classrooms, repair to schools damaged during the riots, elimination of double sessions and platoon systems, and more and better teachers. Steps should also be taken to reduce the high drop-out rate. As it is, students will be forced into a grossly inadequate system.

It is not just through the schools that the government affects the lives of black children. A whole range of oppressive and humiliating laws combine with poverty to make it difficult for black parents to create a stable family life, or even to maintain their sense of dignity in the eyes of their sons and daughters.

One of the white man's legislative measures most bitterly resented by the blacks is the influx control laws, which restrict the movement of blacks from the rural areas to the urban areas, virtually reducing them to the status of prisoners in their own land. These laws require all men and women over sixteen years of age to carry a passbook. Without a passbook, a person cannot obtain work, get married, own a house, or travel—and even with it, before he can do any of these things he must get his passbook stamped with permission from the authorities. A man from the rural areas, if given permission, can work in the urban areas, but only in certain classified jobs: for example, as a garbage collector, a cook, a gardener, or a road digger. Those who go into classified jobs find themselves living in what are called hostels, in the most inhuman conditions. These men cannot have their wives, girlfriends or children to stay with them.

Another hated law devised by the government is the migratory labor law. It is a proven fact that not one of the rural areas is economically viable. The government had to devise the migratory labor law to enable blacks to move at controlled periods to the rich mines to seek work under a contract system. The law forbids men to take their families with them to the mines, fostering the most complicated and cruel social and emotional problems in men who are suddenly bachelors and women who are suddenly grass widows.

Life for blacks from the urban areas is little better. In Soweto the living conditions overall are appalling, except for the lucky few who are rich and can afford to have beautiful houses in Dube, Rockville, a section of Orlando West called Beverly Hills, and a new area being developed called Selection Park. The ordinary basics of civilized life such as street lighting, housing, shopping facilities, and cultural centers are grossly inadequate in Soweto. Only now are shopping centers being built in some parts of the township.

The races continue to drift further and further apart under a government that is not prepared to back down on any of the racial and security laws which are the cause of this state of chaos.

In the tragic South African situation, it has been difficult for the various non-white races—the blacks, the "coloureds" and the Indians—to perceive themselves as one oppressed people, because the country's racial laws are calculated from the old theory of "divide and rule." The riots brought a shock to the government, for black awareness and identification with blacks was registered on a large scale amongst coloureds. In Durban, the Indian students of Westville University boycotted classes in solidarity with fellow blacks. Both in Cape Town and at the University of Western Cape, coloureds demonstrated against the shootings in the black townships of Soweto, Guguletu, and Nyanga. This was the first time that coloured schoolchildren demonstrated in solidarity with the children of Soweto openly on such a scale.

As rioting spread from Soweto throughout the country, it was clear that the blacks were rejecting the whole concept of white rule and its values and norms. This awakening of a people was long overdue.

Yet many black parents are disturbed by the increasing radicalism of their children. Percy Qoboza, editor of the *Post* in Johannesburg (a leading black newspaper, which the government forced to close early in 1981), expressed the problem in an address to the Ikageng Women's Association in April 1979:

> How many times have we heard the anguished cry of fathers and mothers who daily tell us their sons and daughters are only 15 years of age but the political views they express are frightening? Your child shares in your sense of indignity when you are stopped outside your yard and asked to produce your passbook.

Your child shares in your sense of outrage and anger when police arrive in your house in the middle of the night and take you away, throw you into jail without trial, and for weeks, even months, refuse your wife the right to see you.

As the police cars drive off into the night, they leave behind seeds of hatred in the hearts of your small kids. This is the cruelty under which the children have to be brought up in Soweto.

In South Africa, from the moment black children are born they taste oppression. Many of them are forced to become adults at an early age. Often when a child in Soweto reaches one year it is left in the care of its brother or sister, who may be about eight years old, while the mother leaves home as early as 5:00 a.m. to go to work as a domestic in the suburbs of Johannesburg or in a factory. The love that every child needs is rarely given to a black child. Instead, the black mother spends the whole day working and giving all her affection to a white employer's child. By the time the mother gets home she is very tired and there is not enough time, love or care left over for her own children. It is amazing that, out of all these sufferings, so many black children still manage to become normal adults.

The little child left to look after a younger sibling is responsible for cooking, cleaning the house, washing the clothes and paying the house rent. If these chores are not properly done or a slight mistake made, the poor child gets blamed as if he were an adult, not a child. He is only a child when it suits the mother, and is otherwise subject to harsh treatment.

Most black children don't know what toys look like. The toys they know are home-made ones, put together from tomato boxes and wire. Only children from well-to-do homes can afford to have toys from stores.

These babies left in the care of other babies are bound to suffer from numerous diseases, particularly those connected with malnutrition. Even in the rural areas, where mothers stay home but husbands are away for months at a time, you find a lot of malnutrition and cases of the protein-deficiency disease kwashiorkor. The women are unable to cultivate the land because it is so dry, and their husbands send very little money to them to maintain the children.

I remember going to the Transkei in 1976 to do a story on life in the Homelands. In a village called Ngcuka, near Tsolo, east of Umtata, I found a ten-year-old child vomiting in the street. His stomach was painfully distended. I asked his mother what was the matter with him, but she didn't know. He had been eating as usual, but had been vomiting for several days. I took the child and mother to the nearest hospital, where he was examined and marasmus was diagnosed. This is another disease caused by malnutrition. The soft porridge which was all the mother could provide for the child to eat simply did not contain the protein he needed.

In 1979, I did a story on malnutrition in Natal. At the Charles Johnson Memorial Hospital in Nqutu there were five wards of children suffering from kwashiorkor. That particular part of the country has the largest percentage of children with the disease, but in the whole country it is only black children who suffer from kwashiorkor. South Africa has no reason to have so many cases with all the food it exports. Instead of being exported, food should be given to the needy people in the country.

South Africa is one of the few countries in the civilized world where child labor is still an issue. We do have a Children's Act, but it protects only the white child. Black children are not protected, and often their families' poverty forces them to work, at wages that are cruelly exploitative.

In urban areas, children are employed by the newspaper industry to sell papers. Both the English and the Afrikaans companies employ and grossly underpay them. They start to assemble as early as 3:00 a.m. At 5:00 a.m. they are taken to different points to begin their round of selling. After selling the morning papers, they take a short break before starting on the afternoon shift. When the afternoon takings have been counted, they are brought home. At the earliest, they get home by 8:00 p.m.

The situation on the farms is even worse. In an agricultural country like ours, it is perfectly natural and healthy that children should help with light tasks around the farms, but there are certain guidelines that should surely be complied with. First of all, I do not believe that very young children should be separated from their parents for long periods to work on the farms. Secondly, farmers who employ children during harvesting should take the greatest care to see that they do only the very lightest work; that they do not have to work long hours; and that they be given nutritious food and enough water. And most important, they should not be allowed to work at the expense of their education. All of these guidelines are consistently ignored on the farms of South Africa.

Between 1958 and 1967, and again in 1979, I was drawn closer to child farm labor issues through my work with *Drum Magazine*. During these years I visited a number of farms in the Eastern Transvaal region that produced potatoes, maize, pumpkin, tomatoes and other vegetables.

Some of the children I spoke to on my visits complained bitterly about their wages, food, accommodations and working conditions. The youngest child I spoke to said she was nine years old. Little boys and girls who should be at school or at home under their mother's care are digging potatoes and loading pumpkins for white farmers in the Eastern Transvaal. Some of the children are recruited from far-off Sekhukhuneland, the Transkei, Ciskei, Bophutatswana, and Weenen in Natal. Many come under a nine-month contract. The farmers bring them from their homes at the start of the nine months, and take them back at the end; they have neither the money for transport nor any free time to go home for a visit during the time of the contract. Others are from the local townships. Children are paid the equivalent of about 50¢ a day.

Farmers provide transportation for the local children to be picked up from their homes as early as 6:30 a.m. and brought back after sunset. On the job, these children are provided with porridge, no meat.

Farm-working children are supervised by a black foreman. This foreman has orders to report any strangers discovered on the farm talking to workers. On a number of occasions I was told that I should not talk to the child laborers or take photographs, but sometimes I managed to convince the foreman to let me talk to them and take photographs. On other farms, I was simply told that no strangers were allowed and I should leave immediately.

In 1979, I went to the Eastern Transvaal in the Delmas, Leslie, Bethal, Kinross and Caroline areas to conduct a survey of migrant farm laborers on the contract system. At an old dilapidated white farmhouse in the Delmas area lived a group of eighty Xhosa laborers from Lady Frere, ranging in age from twelve to forty. These men, women, boys and girls were living under appalling conditions. They had arrived in February of 1979 to work on a farm belonging to a man named Sam Hirschowitz. When recruited, they were told that they would be paid good money and have good accommodations and food. "Our travel documents were taken away from us and given to the farmer for safe-keeping," Mrs. M. Nohombi Matyulweni told me. "If we want to leave before the contract expires, the farmer refuses to give our documents back, so we are made to work until we have completed our contract. If we should get ill, our money is deducted for the number of days absent, and you are not taken to the doctor immediately. It is only when you become seriously ill that the boss boy takes you to see a doctor. The farmer pays for our medical expenses and later deducts it out of our salary. . . . Some children have gone back to their homes in the Transkei, leaving behind their documents and their pay. If I had my way, I would run away."

None of the children I spoke to had ever been to school. They all lived in the dilapidated farmhouse, which was filthy. One of the boys described it as a "cattle corral." "We can't even see the cement flooring because of the caked dust," he said.

A typical farmhouse, complete with veranda during its better days, it had no doors or windows when the laborers came to live in it. There was no furniture in the house except for the foreman's room. Some of the workers, mostly young boys, lived in an outhouse not far from the main house. It was about 10 feet long by 8 feet wide. There were no electric lights or running water. The water was drawn from a stream some distance away; for light, they relied on the sun, diesel lamps, and cooking fires. Improvised mattresses were made from sacks and other material, including dirty, ragged blankets and articles of clothing. The floors were cracked and littered with mealie husks, cobs and dirt. During my visit to this farm three young girls gave birth in that filthy farmhouse without running water or any medication. After seeing this place, I could no longer contain myself. I drove back to Johannesburg and gathered clothing and food from friends in the city. I was able to feed the laborers for about three weeks before they returned home. I also got a doctor to visit the farm with me. Dr. Selma Browdie was amazed and shocked when she spoke to some of the children in their filthy home.

In the Weenen district in Natal, children of as young as six are collected by trucks in the morning and taken to the farms. They are not provided with any food—they have to bring their own. These children work from 7:00 a.m. to 5:30 p.m. Some are paid in money, others are given potatoes or tomatoes. One of the farmers in the district said it was better for him to employ children than adults because children can bend for a long time. Harvesting and planting require bending. My colleague and I asked the farmer why the children were not at school; did he not realize that it is an offense to employ children? His answer was: "It is not an offense to employ black children. I'm doing them a favor by giving them work. Without work they would starve." During the summer months it is unbearably hot; yet these children spent the whole day exposed to the sun.

In some cases children are made to work for land tenancy. This means they work on the fields to enable their parents to stay on the farms. Parents who have two children will have one child work for six months while the other one is at school, and vice versa.

My last venture into the farms was in Delmas. My colleague and I went up to a farm, but before we could enter the gate, which was out of bounds for visitors, the farmer called on us to stop. He was followed by a young white policeman. They came up to us demanding to see our passes and wanting to know what we were doing in the area. I explained that we were doing a story on child farm labor, and pointed out that we were not on anybody's property. The farmer then pulled out a revolver, threatening us and insisting that we wait in the company of the policeman while he went to get a witness. He got into his car and drove off. I asked the policeman whether we were under arrest. He said no. We left immediately, knowing that the policeman would not be able to protect us if the farmers gave us a beating.

In the whole of South Africa you will not find any white children working on farms. The system is meant to kill the black child spiritually, morally and mentally at a very tender age. By the time black children reach adulthood, they have nothing much left.

South Africa has silenced nearly all the organizations that were outlets for black protest. The students' organizations were almost the only ones left, and in 1977 the government banned the South African Students' Movement (SASM) and its offshoot, the Soweto Students' Representative Council (SSRC), for their part in the Soweto riots.

In May 1979, judgment was passed in the trial of the "Soweto Eleven": the judge found eleven members of the SSRC, some of whom were only sixteen at the time of the riots, guilty of sedition. They had already been in jail for over two years. The judge took into account their youth and the time already served, and let seven of them off with five-year suspended sentences. Perhaps he also feared the anger of the black people throughout the country who were watching the trial anxiously. The longest jail sentence he gave was four years.

But the ones whose sentences were suspended did not get off free. They will have to tread carefully for the length of their sentences—if they offend the law in any way during that time, they may have to serve the whole sentence in jail after all. It is not always easy for a black person in South Africa to avoid breaking the law. Certainly, it will be difficult for them to be involved in any kind of politics.

Meanwhile every year more black children are old enough to be angry. Their elders, the ones who ought to be leaders, are all in prison, or banished. The children's anger will keep boiling up without direction.

Children continue dying to save the world. The tragedy is that South African laws are made for the benefit of the white minority and to persecute the black majority. Let our children grow up like other children of the civilized world. The future of South Africa lies in the hands of the children. Without children there is no tomorrow.

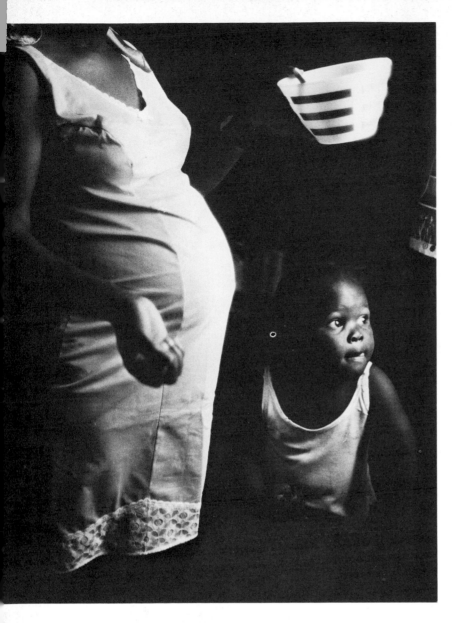

A black childhood begins. Left, a housewife in Soweto waiting for her second child. Below, a mother meets her newborn at the Johnson Memorial Hospital in Nqutu, Natal.

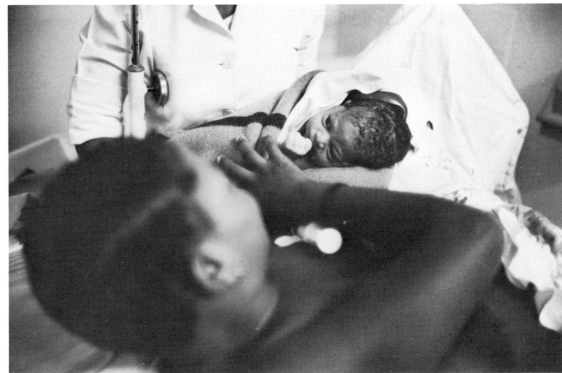

The children in these pictures are the granddaughters of Nelson Mandela, the black leader who has been in prison in Robben Island since 1962. Zenani Dlamini, the girls' mother, lives in Swaziland with her husband, but for both births she traveled to the remote corner of South Africa to which her mother, Winnie Mandela, has been banished. Winnie Mandela had to get special permission to come to the hospital.

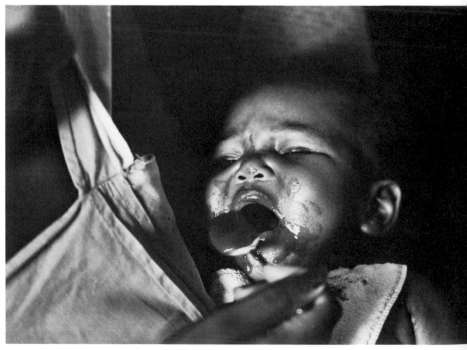

This child is being baptized into the Zion Christian Church, one of the most popular churches, in a river that runs through Soweto.

Most of the houses in Alexandra Township have no
running water. You have to empty the water into the
street when you have finished washing.

I photographed the child running to school near my home in Diepkloof, Soweto. Above, a birthday party in one of the better-off families of Soweto.

There are no government-run kindergartens for black children, but some private kindergartens get by on fees paid by parents and with charitable support from white businesses. I took these pictures at a school of this kind, in Alexandra Township. Above, saying grace before lunch. The children in the picture above right were putting on a play for the school's benefactors.

Most of the government schools for black children are overcrowded. The boy in the picture above left was reciting a poem for his class. The class is held outside whenever possible because the school building is so cramped. The school shown above, in Winterveld, north of Pretoria, is built of corrugated iron. In the picture below left a teacher and a student from a white school present a gift of oranges and paraffin heaters to the students of a school in Alexandra Township. It is quite common for a white school to "adopt" a black school as a charitable cause.

At a school in Soweto, several classes must be held in
one room.

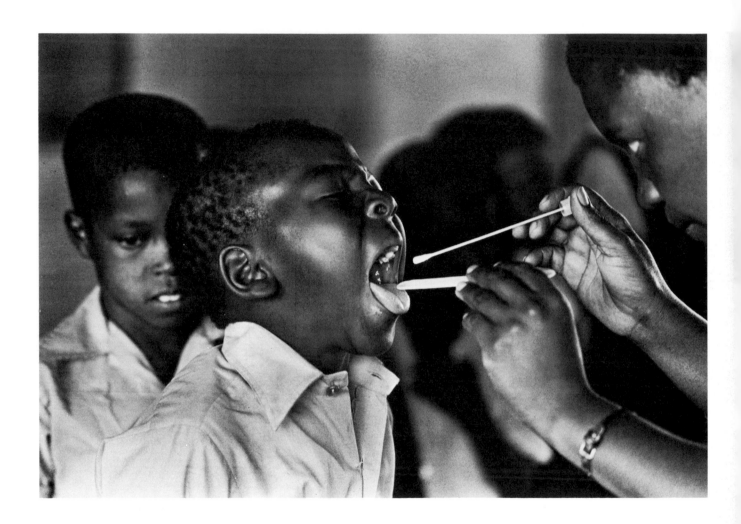

This child was having his throat checked at his school in Soweto when there was the threat of an epidemic. The people at right are waiting at the surgery of a black doctor in Hammenskraal, north of Pretoria. Even though a black doctor's patients cannot pay high fees, it is usually better for him to have a private practice than to work in a hospital, because hospitals pay black doctors poorly—much less than white doctors.

I took these pictures in the country, in Natal. The children in the picture at left have swollen bellies because they don't get enough protein in their diet. The picture above shows a mother taking her sick baby to the doctor—a long, slow journey.

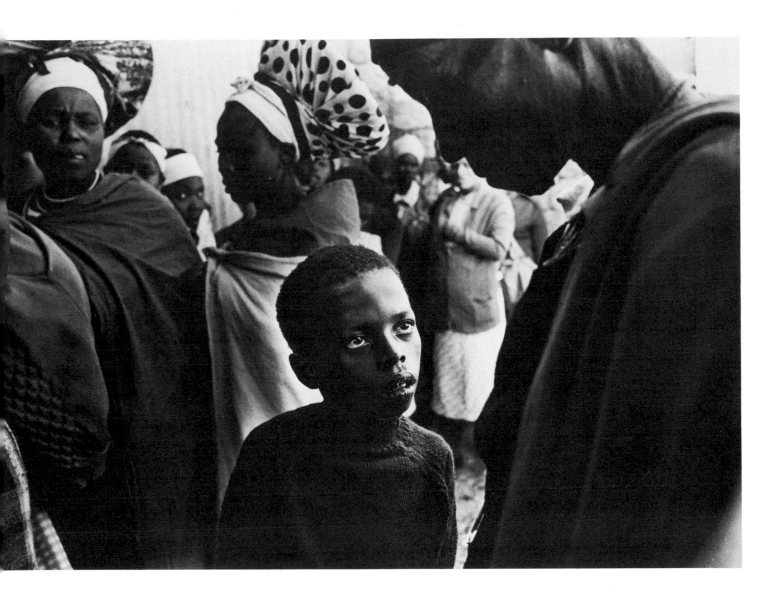

At the outpatients clinic of the Charles S. Johnson Memorial Hospital in Nqutu, Natal. The child at left was being weighed, as part of her medical examination. The boy above was waiting in the line for treatment. Later he was admitted to the hospital to be treated for kwashiorkor.

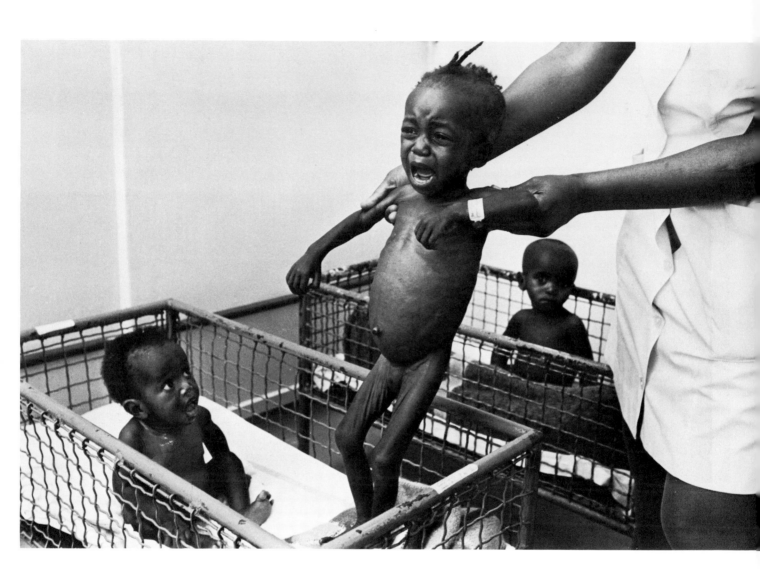

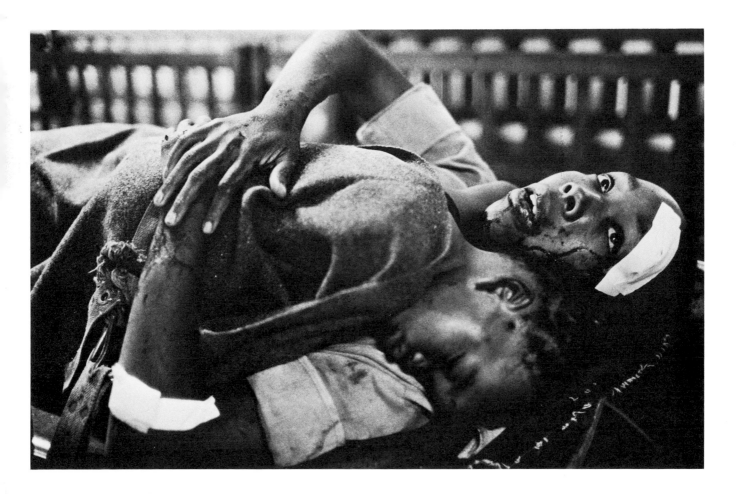

The little girl opposite had been admitted to the Charles S. Johnson Memorial Hospital with kwashiorkor. The mother and daughter shown above had been in a bus accident on a Saturday night and were waiting for medical attention at the Baragwanath Hospital in Soweto. This is the largest black hospital in South Africa, and it is a good one, but it is understaffed.

The children above were gathering firewood for their families. At right, on a cold winter's day some children huddle around the brazier, which is the only source of heat in their home.

Black children have to be resourceful. The boy above
right was gathering scrap to make toys. Above, a game
of street football, Soweto.

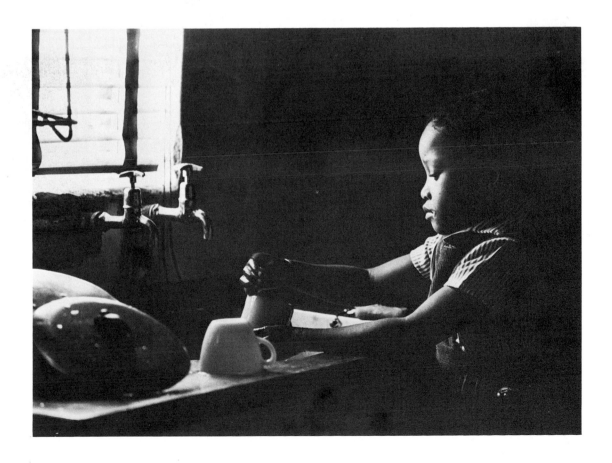

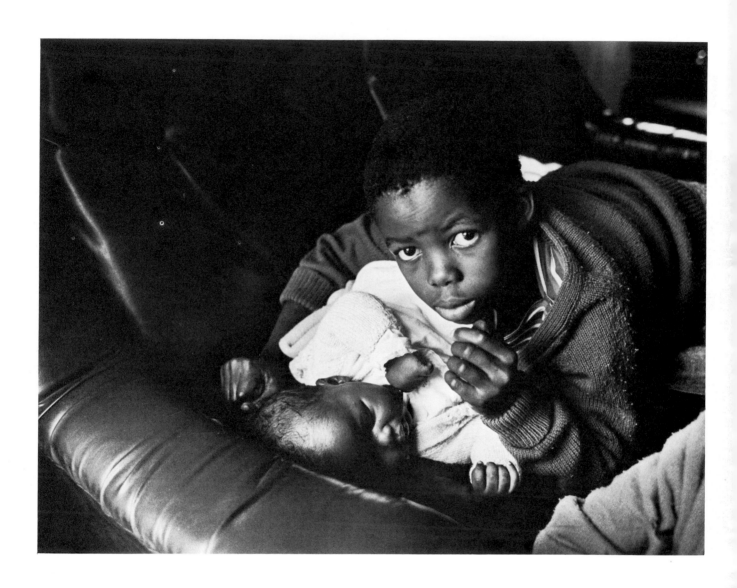

The boy above was looking after his sister while their mother was at work. At right, a wedding celebration in Diepkloof, Soweto. The children don't wait to be invited to join the festivities.

The children above, photographed in Alexandra Township, had set up their own small braziers in tin cans. At right, an enterprising businessman in Diepkloof set up a trampoline for children—they paid 2¢ for a given number of jumps. The setting sun was filtered through the smoke of the fires cooking the evening meal.

In the fifties the government began a program of clearing black slums—and rebuilding them as areas for whites only. Sometimes temporary relocation camps are provided, but often the black people living in the area simply have to find somewhere else to live. I took this picture in Sophiatown, a black district in Johannesburg which no longer exists. The houses were already being torn down, though this child and her sister, who was playing nearby, still lived there. Sophiatown was rebuilt with a new Afrikaans name: Triomph. I photographed the determined child at right in Edenvale, Johannesburg, in 1967. A little while later Edenvale too was torn down and rebuilt as a white area.

Modderdam was a settlement of "squatters" in Cape-town—that is, of black people who were living in the city without permits to be in the white area. White employers encourage the presence of squatters, by hiring them at higher wages than they could get in the Homelands—but much lower than blacks with permits can expect. Every now and then the police crack down on squatters. The people in Modderdam were forced to move and the homes they had built were bulldozed. The child above was having his last meal before the police arrived. The boy at left had just been moved with his family to Mafeking, Cape Province, from another district that had been declared white. In the circumstances it was too much for him to bear that he had dropped his mug of milk.

I took the picture at left at a transit camp that had
been set up for families that were forced to move.
Above, a family of squatters in Johannesburg, making
their home in an abandoned truck. When squatters are
evicted they are supposed to return to their "Homelands"—but often they have been living in the city for
years (or, like this child, were born there) and have no
connection with the rural areas any more. They are
forced into an underground life.

Juvenile delinquency is common in Johannesburg. The kids above were sniffing glue. At right, a traffic police-man grabs a pickpocket.

It's not unusual to see children like the one at left begging in downtown Johannesburg. I took the picture above in the market in Meadowlands, Soweto. The boy is working for his parents, selling the intestines of various animals—delicious, if properly prepared.

The boy pictured above was working in an Indian family's fruit shop at the Indian Market in Johannesburg. South Africa's Indians are notorious for exploiting the labor of black children even more than the whites do. I talked to the homeless youth at right and learned that he had been brought to Johannesburg from his home in Rustenberg three years before by an Indian family to work in their store. A little while later he was fired. He had no money to get home to his family, and had never been able to find another job. He lives by scavenging.

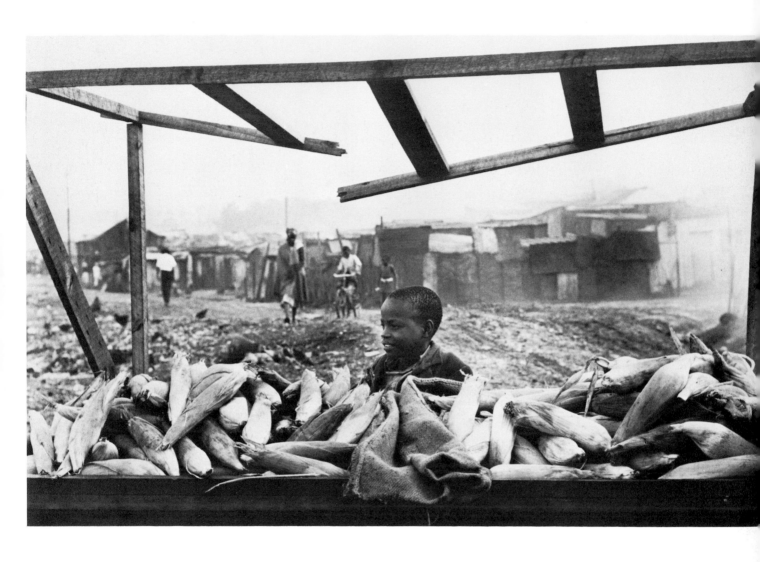

Above, tending his parents' vegetable stand in Edenvale. Opposite, in Volksrust, East Transvaal, a country family heads home after a day buying and selling in the city.

There are hundreds of children working long days as newsboys in Johannesburg. The truck picks them up from their homes any time from 3:00 a.m. on.

The boys above were playing dice on their break. Below left, turning in their takings at the end of the day.

In Weenen, Natal, the farmers employ children who live nearby to work in the fields. At left, the truck was picking the children up at about 6 a.m. The children above had just been dropped off near their homes at the end of the day. The girl's pail held her lunch.

I took these pictures in the potato fields in East Transvaal.

These youngsters were working on a sugar plantation in Natal.

I spent a long time in Delmas photographing the maize harvest and getting to know the workers.

The eighteen-year-old boy's leg, above, was pierced by
a maize stalk and went septic. There was no medicine
on the farm, and it was difficult to keep the wound
clean. I took this picture eight months later.

These pictures show what the boys' dormitories were like on two farms in Delmas. The one shown above at least had a window. For the pictures at right I had to use a flash because there was no light except for the makeshift paraffin lamps the boys made. Above right, I brought Dr. Selma Browdie from Johannesburg to see the farm. She found it hard to believe how bad the conditions were.

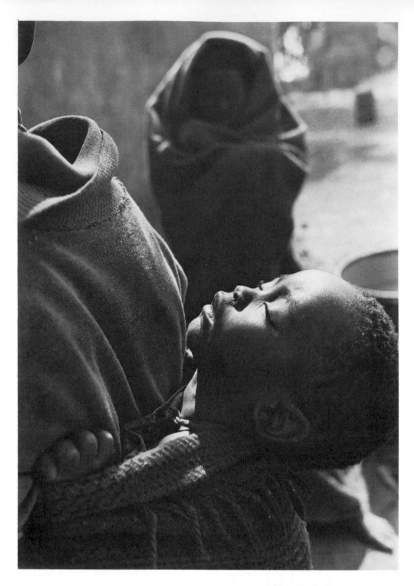

The nineteen-year-old girl at left gave birth on the farm, with no medical help. She had no clothes for the baby—I gave her the blankets myself. She went straight back to working in the fields. (The white powder on her face is a home-made salve for sunburn.) The owner of this farm pays one of the women to look after all the babies while the others are at work. There are farms where women have to work with their babies on their backs, like the one above left.

Above, meals on the farm are prepared outside on a
smoky fire of cow-dung. The child with a basin on her
head is gathering dung for fuel. Below left, the usual
meal: soft porridge.

There was some time on the farm for recreation. The
boy at left made his guitar from an oil can. Above, a
more traditional musical instrument.

One of the workers took the picture of me at above left after I brought food and blankets to the farm. I brought them some bread on the last day of their contract, below left, because they had nothing to eat on the nine-hour journey to their home in the Transkei. The white man on the right in the picture is the driver. Above, the workers celebrated their return home.

I took these pictures in Soweto on 17 June 1976, the first day of the riots. The children at above right were setting fire to cartons of beer from one of the government-owned beer halls, which are the only source of alcohol in the black townships. The group in the picture below right were stopping cars and taxis to ask drivers and passengers for support in the protest.

Above, looters as well as protesters raided the beer halls. Right, as the riots continued, a boy was killed by the police in Mamelodi-Pretoria.

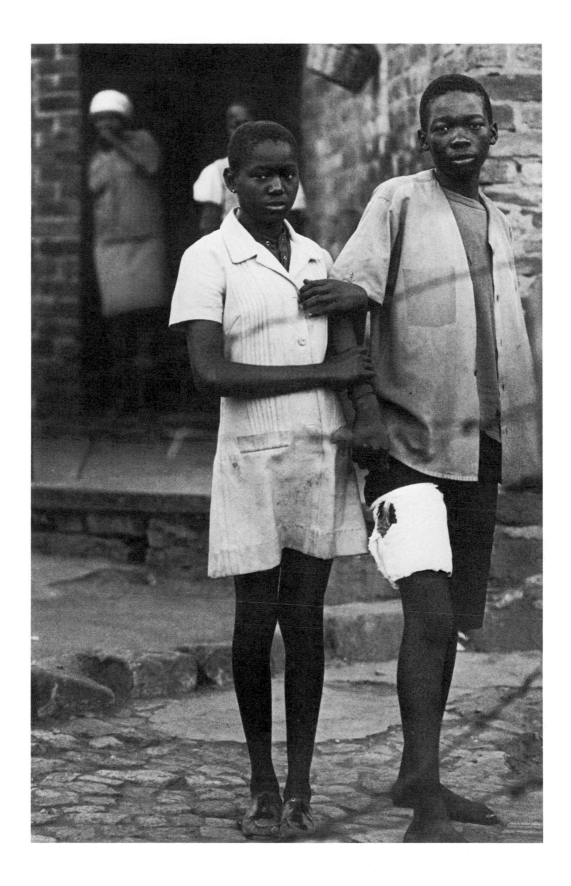

I took the pictures opposite at the funeral of a student who was killed by the police in Soweto in 1976. The riots spread almost across the country. The boy shown above with his sister was shot by the police in the small coal-mining town of Witbank in the Eastern Transvaal.

On the anniversary of the 1976 riots new protests erupted and more lives were lost. I took these pictures at the funeral of a student who died in the 1977 unheavals.

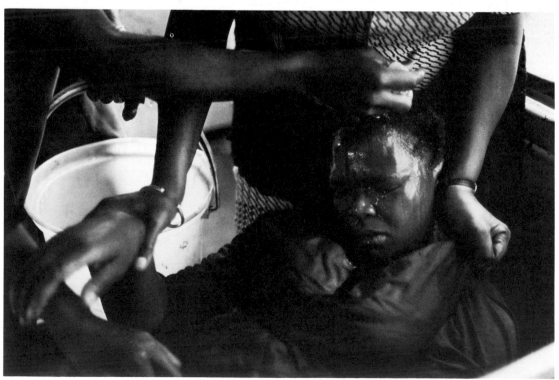

It happened again in 1978. A funeral for one of the students who died that year ended in confusion when the police used tear gas to disrupt the students' protests. Everybody ran blindly for the buses, and the girl at left fainted from the gas.

In 1978, Robert Sobukwe, one-time leader of the forbidden Pan-Africanist Congress, died. He had been banned since the 1960s, but had not been forgotten. There was a march to his graveside, above. Fearful of riots, the authorities instructed the police to exercise special restraint during the demonstration. The disturbance at the funeral came not from the police but from a dispute between the radical students and Gatsha Buthelezi, leader of a Zulu organization based in Natal which favors the continuation of the Homelands for the blacks. Buthelezi was to speak at the funeral. Students tried to prevent him, and in the scuffle the boy in the picture at right was wounded by a bullet.

Soweto 1978. There were not enough buses to take everyone to the funeral of one of the students who had died in a demonstration, and many of us walked the four miles to the cemetery. My colleague William Nkosi took the picture of me and the children on that march.

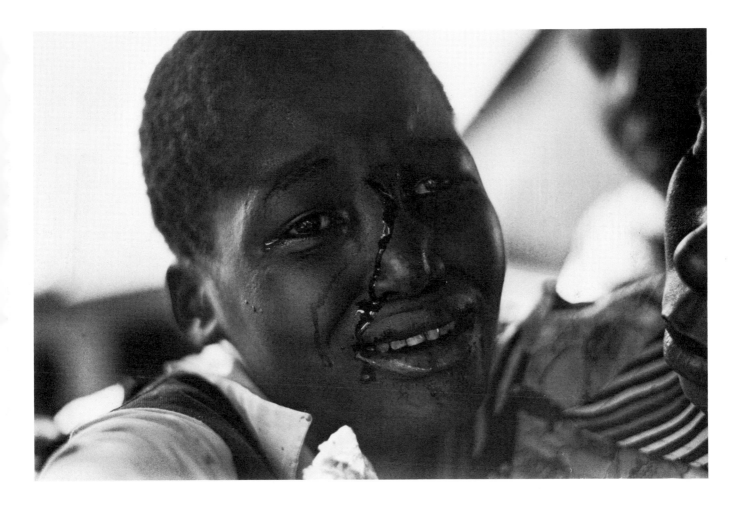

In 1979, the freedom fighter Solomon Mahlangu was hanged for murder at a prison in Pretoria. Students demonstrated outside the cemetery as they waited for the prison authorities to deliver Mahlangu's body for burial. The girl above was hit by a policeman's truncheon.

On the last day of the trial of the "Soweto Eleven" the accused filed into the dock singing the anthem, "Azania my beloved home, I will fight for my country until it goes free." Some of them had already been in detention for more than two years. The emotion of the moment when they received sentence, and could at last see an end to their captivity, was overwhelming. Susan Mthembu (above left) and Seth Mazibuko greet their relatives before going back to serve their sentences.

The grave of Hector Peterson, the thirteen-year-old boy
who was the first to die in the Soweto riots.

A NOTE ABOUT THE AUTHOR

Born in Johannesburg in 1932, Peter Magubane began his career as a photographer on *Drum* magazine in 1956. In 1965, he became a staff member of the *Rand Daily Mail*, a Johannesburg newspaper. His experiences over twenty years as the only major black South African news photographer—including arrests, solitary confinement, banning orders—are recounted in his first book, *Magubane's South Africa*. Since the publication of that book he has completed photographic assignments in various parts of the world for such magazines as *Time* and *Geo*, and has worked in television news. He has also had a number of exhibitions in the United States and Europe. He still maintains his home in Diepkloof, a section of the black township of Soweto outside Johannesburg.

A NOTE ON THE TYPE

The text of this book was set in the film version of Optima, a type face designed by Hermann Zapf from 1952–1955 and issued in 1958. In designing Optima, Zapf created a truly new type form—a cross between the classic roman and a sans-serif face. So delicate are the stresses and balances in Optima that it rivals sans-serif faces in clarity and freshness and old-style faces in variety and interest.

Composed by Maryland Linotype Composition
Company, Inc., Baltimore, Maryland
Printed and bound by The Murray Printing Company,
Westford, Massachusetts
Designed by Anthea Lingeman